# Manifest Destiny
## The Dream of a New Nation

**Lorraine Harrison**

NEW YORK

Published in 2017 by The Rosen Publishing Group, Inc.
29 East 21st Street, New York, NY 10010

Editor: Katie Kawa
Book Design: Samantha DeMartin

Photo Credits: Cover https://commons.wikimedia.org/wiki/File:Samuel_Colman_-_Ship_of_the_Plains.jpg; p. 4 https://commons.wikimedia.org/wiki/File:American_progress.JPG; p. 5 Encyclopaedia Britannica/Universal Images Group/Getty Images; p. 6 GraphicaArtis/Archive Photos/Getty Images; pp. 7, 10, 15 MPI/Archive Photos/ Getty Images; p. 9 https://commons.wikimedia.org/wiki/File:Cherokee-removal-sign-tn1.jpg; p. 11 Universal History Archive/Universal Images Group/Getty Images; p. 13 UniversalImagesGroup/Universal Images Group/ Getty Images; p. 14 https://commons.wikimedia.org/wiki/File:Map_of_Mexico_1847.jpg; p. 16 https://commons. wikimedia.org/wiki/File:The_Last_Spike_1869.jpg; p. 17 Culture Club/Hulton Archive/Getty Images; p. 19 Charles Phelps Cushing/ClassicStock/Archive Photos/Getty Images; p. 20 Underwood Archives/Archive Photos/Getty Images; p. 21 Maximus256/Shutterstock.com.

**Library of Congress Cataloging-in-Publication Data**

Names: Harrison, Lorraine, 1959- author.
Title: Manifest destiny : the dream of a new nation / Lorraine Harrison.
Description: New York : PowerKids Press, [2016] | Series: Spotlight on
   American history | Includes index.
Identifiers: LCCN 2015048098 | ISBN 9781508149521 (pbk.) | ISBN 9781508149392 (library bound) | ISBN
9781508149187 (6 pack)
Subjects: LCSH: Manifest Destiny. | United States--Territorial
   expansion--Juvenile literature. | West (U.S.)--History--19th
   century--Juvenile literature.
Classification: LCC E179.5 .H265 2016 | DDC 978/.02--dc23
LC record available at http://lccn.loc.gov/2015048098

Manufactured in the United States of America

CPSIA Compliance Information: Batch #BS16PK: For further information contact Rosen Publishing, New York, New York at 1-800-237-9932.

# CONTENTS

FROM SEA TO SHINING SEA . . . . . . . . . . . . 4

A BIG STEP WESTWARD . . . . . . . . . . . . . . . 6

WHO OWNS THE LAND? . . . . . . . . . . . . . . . 8

EYES ON OREGON . . . . . . . . . . . . . . . . . . . . 10

"FIFTY-FOUR FORTY OR FIGHT!" . . . . . . . 12

EXPANSION BY FORCE . . . . . . . . . . . . . . . . 14

CONNECTING EAST AND WEST . . . . . . . . 16

A NEW DESTINY . . . . . . . . . . . . . . . . . . . . . . 18

ALASKA AND HAWAII . . . . . . . . . . . . . . . . . 20

A SPECIAL DESTINY . . . . . . . . . . . . . . . . . . 22

GLOSSARY . . . . . . . . . . . . . . . . . . . . . . . . . . . 23

INDEX . . . . . . . . . . . . . . . . . . . . . . . . . . . . . . . 24

PRIMARY SOURCE LIST . . . . . . . . . . . . . . . 24

WEBSITES . . . . . . . . . . . . . . . . . . . . . . . . . . . 24

JAN 3 - 2017

# FROM SEA TO SHINING SEA

The United States didn't always stretch "from sea to shining sea" as it does today. When it first became an independent nation, its people lived close to the Atlantic Ocean. However, it didn't take long before they began to dream of heading west.

*The idea of Manifest Destiny was expressed in popular works of art in the 19th century, such as this 1872 painting by John Gast titled* American Progress.

By the 19th century, many Americans had their sights set on the Pacific Ocean. They believed the United States was **destined** to reach from the Atlantic Ocean to the Pacific Ocean. Americans thought it was their God-given right to settle the land across the North American continent and even beyond its boundaries. This became known as Manifest Destiny.

*John L. O'Sullivan*

It's believed that the first use of that phrase occurred in 1845, when magazine editor John L. O'Sullivan wrote that it was "the fulfillment of our manifest destiny to overspread the continent...." The era of Manifest Destiny had begun, and it wouldn't end until Americans had settled "from sea to shining sea."

# A BIG STEP WESTWARD

Although the phrase "Manifest Destiny" wasn't used until 1845, the idea that the United States was destined to expand had been a part of its history since colonial times. The 13 colonies themselves were an experiment in westward expansion for Britain. Once those colonies became states, the people who lived in them continued to push westward.

In 1803, President Thomas Jefferson bought the Louisiana Territory from France in what's now called the Louisiana Purchase. This was the young

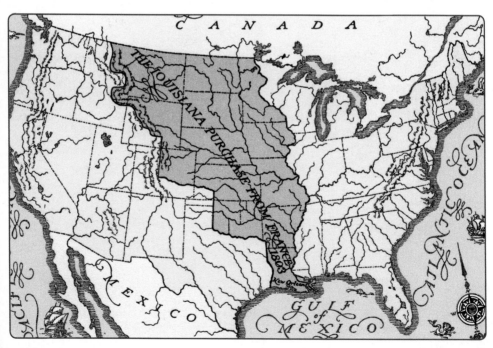

*This map shows the lands acquired in the Louisiana Purchase.*

*President Jefferson hoped Lewis and Clark's expedition would discover a water route to the Pacific Ocean. Even in the earliest days of westward expansion, the president was interested in getting from one ocean to another.*

nation's first big step westward, as it acquired lands from the Mississippi River to the Rocky Mountains.

In May 1804, Meriwether Lewis and William Clark set out with a small group known as the Corps of Discovery to explore the lands acquired in the Louisiana Purchase. On their journey, they met with many Native Americans. Each time they met a new Native American group, they told them their lands now belonged to the United States.

# WHO OWNS THE LAND?

As settlers began to **migrate** to the new lands acquired through the Louisiana Purchase, they came into contact with Native Americans who'd been living on those lands for centuries. Conflicts often arose because both groups viewed land ownership in very different ways.

This difference in ideas often led to violence between Native Americans and settlers. The settlers fought for the land they believed they were entitled to, while the Native Americans fought to continue to live on their homelands. Both sides suffered losses, but the Native Americans lost the most. Diseases and deadly conflicts caused Native American populations to decrease sharply, which made it harder for them to fight back against settlers and the U.S. government. By the time Manifest Destiny was realized, most Native Americans were living on **reservations**.

CHEROKEE REMOVAL MEMORIAL PARK

NU·NO·DU·NA·TLO·Hi·LU  The Trail Where They Cried

From 1838 to 1839, the U.S. government forced thousands of Cherokees to leave their lands in the southeastern United States to migrate to Indian Territory in what's now Oklahoma. This journey became known as the Trail of Tears because at least 4,000 Cherokee people are believed to have died along the way. The Cherokee Removal Park in Tennessee, shown here, is dedicated to the memory of those forced to take part in the Trail of Tears.

# EYES ON OREGON

Clashes between settlers and Native Americans became more frequent in the mid-1800s, because more settlers were moving farther west. Many settlers had their eyes fixed on Oregon Country, which stretched from the Rocky Mountains to the Pacific Ocean. It included land that's now the states of Oregon, Idaho, and Washington, as well as the Canadian **province** of British Columbia. Parts of what's now Wyoming and Montana were also considered part of Oregon Country. Both the United States and Britain claimed lands in this region.

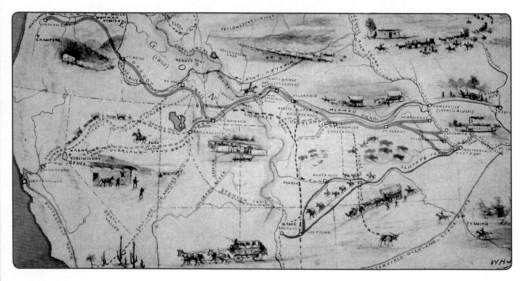

*Oregon Trail*

*As more Americans came to Oregon Country on the Oregon Trail, shown here, leaders began to work to set a clear border between American and British lands in the region.*

Oregon Country became the center of discussions about Manifest Destiny because of its location between the lands of the Louisiana Purchase and the Pacific Ocean. Those who believed in Manifest Destiny saw it as the connecting piece needed for America to reach from one ocean to another.

Oregon Country became especially valuable as more and more settlers traveled through it on the **Oregon Trail**. Whole families began to travel in covered wagons to Oregon Country, hoping for a better life in the West.

# "FIFTY-FOUR FORTY OR FIGHT!"

The U.S. government worked to achieve the promise of Manifest Destiny in different ways. One way was by **negotiation**, which is how the United States came to control its share of Oregon Country.

While the United States and Britain agreed to a joint occupation of Oregon Country in 1818, by the 1840s, leaders began calling for a set border between the two countries in this region. President James K. Polk was vocal in his belief in expanding the United States across North America, and he wanted to acquire as much land in Oregon Country as possible.

Polk wanted to set the border with Britain at the 54 degree, 40 minute **latitude** line. However, U.S. leaders and British leaders ultimately settled on the 49th parallel, or latitude line, as the border, with Britain getting all of Vancouver Island in the deal. The treaty establishing this border was **ratified** in June 1846. Oregon became a U.S. territory that same year, and it became a U.S. state in 1859.

It's believed that when Polk, shown here, ran for president in 1844, one of his campaign slogans was "Fifty-four forty or fight!" This referred to where he wanted to set the border with Britain in Oregon Country. However, other U.S. leaders didn't want to fight with Britain over the border, so the 49th parallel was used instead of the 54 degree, 40 minute line.

# EXPANSION BY FORCE

The dream of Manifest Destiny wasn't achieved through negotiation alone. In some cases, the United States expanded by force. The clearest example of this was the U.S.-Mexican War, which took place between 1846 and 1848.

One year before Oregon became a territory, the United States **annexed** Texas. While Oregon's borders were set peacefully, the same wasn't true for Texas.

*This map was used during treaty negotiations between the United States and Mexico.*

*Zachary Taylor, shown here, was known as a hero of the U.S.-Mexican War. He became president after Polk's term ended in 1849.*

In 1846, President Polk sent U.S. soldiers into **disputed** lands along the Rio Grande, which is a river that the United States claimed was the border between Texas and Mexico. On April 25, 1846, fighting broke out between U.S. troops and Mexican troops in this region. The U.S.-Mexican War had begun.

The war ended on February 2, 1848, with the signing of the Treaty of Guadalupe Hidalgo. The United States acquired Mexican lands in what are now the states of California, Nevada, Utah, Arizona, New Mexico, Colorado, and Texas. The dream of Manifest Destiny had become a reality.

# CONNECTING EAST AND WEST

Once the dream of Manifest Destiny was realized, the next dream became connecting the nation with a transcontinental railroad, or a railroad that crossed the entire continent of North America.

This new goal required the acquisition of more Mexican lands. These lands came under the control of the United States through the Gadsden Purchase.

*Railroads allowed Americans to travel across the new lands the United States acquired during the 19th century. They played an important part in the settlement and growth of the West.*

*Shown here is a freight train traveling on the Union Pacific Railroad, which was half of the first transcontinental railroad in the United States.*

This purchase was negotiated by James Gadsden, who was the U.S. minister to Mexico, and Antonio de Santa Anna, who was the Mexican president. Once the two men signed a treaty on December 30, 1853, the United States gained lands in what's now southern Arizona and New Mexico.

On May 10, 1869, the Union Pacific Railroad and the Central Pacific Railroad met at Promontory Summit, Utah, marking the completion of the first transcontinental railroad. Soon after, construction began on the Southern Pacific Railroad, which ran through lands acquired in the Gadsden Purchase.

# A NEW DESTINY

With the start of the **American Civil War** on April 12, 1861, any plans to continue to expand the United States beyond its current borders were put on hold. The era of Manifest Destiny seemed to be over. However, a new era of expansion was right around the corner.

In the late 1800s, influential Americans believed the United States should not only continue to expand, but should also become a world power. The first steps toward this new Manifest Destiny were taken with the Spanish-American War, which took place in 1898.

The United States won the war, and Spain's time as a colonial power in the Americas came to an end. Following the war, Spain gave up Guam and Puerto Rico to the United States. The United States also paid $20 million to take over for Spain as ruler of the Philippines. The young nation was on its way to becoming a new world power.

The Spanish-American War helped the United States grow into the world power it is today.

# ALASKA AND HAWAII

The last two U.S. states—Alaska and Hawaii—are examples of the ways Manifest Destiny remained alive many years after people first began dreaming of expanding the borders of the United States. Alaska was purchased from Russia for $7.2 million on March 30, 1867. However, many Americans didn't approve of the purchase at first. They called it "Seward's **Folly**" after the man who negotiated

*Shown here is a man searching for gold during one of the gold rushes that brought new settlers to Alaska.*

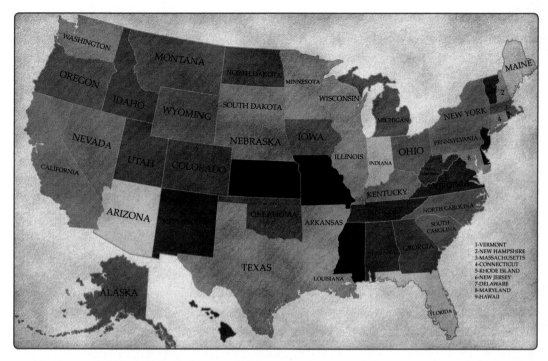

*Alaska and Hawaii both became U.S. states in 1959. They represented the push to continue to expand America into new frontiers.*

the purchase, Secretary of State William Seward. That all changed, however, when gold was discovered in Alaska and the surrounding areas in the late 1800s.

Hawaii was acquired during the new phase of Manifest Destiny in the 1890s. The islands had a ruler, Queen Liliuokalani, and President Grover Cleveland didn't believe in removing her from power. However, the queen was overthrown by powerful Americans living in Hawaii, and a **republic** was formed for a short time. Hawaii was annexed during William McKinley's presidency in 1898 and became a U.S. territory.

# A SPECIAL DESTINY

When John L. O'Sullivan first used the words "Manifest Destiny," he wasn't trying to create a new concept. He was simply trying to state what many Americans had always believed: They had a God-given purpose to spread their way of life across the North American continent. Little did he know that "Manifest Destiny" would soon become a term that would define an entire period of American history.

During the 19th century, the United States experienced a time of rapid growth through many different means—from peaceful negotiations to deadly wars. When that century was over, the nation stretched from the Atlantic Ocean to the Pacific Ocean and beyond. Manifest Destiny, which had once been only a dream, had been realized.

This belief in a special destiny for the United States would continue to be a driving force as the nation grew into a world power. Now, America's influence is felt not just "from sea to shining sea" but around the globe.

# GLOSSARY

**American Civil War (uh-MEHR-uh-kuhn SIH-vuhl WOR):** A war in the United States between the North and South over slavery and other issues.

**annex (AAN-ehks):** To add land to a country or state.

**destined (DEHS-tuhnd):** Meant to be or meant to happen.

**disputed (dih-SPYOOT-tuhd):** Fought over.

**folly (FAH-lee):** A foolish act or idea.

**latitude (LAA-tih-tood):** Distance north or south of the equator measured in degrees and minutes.

**migrate (MY-grayt):** To move from one place to another.

**negotiation (nih-go-shee-AY-shuhn):** A formal discussion between two people trying to reach an agreement.

**Oregon Trail (OR-ih-guhn TRAYL):** A land route that ran from Independence, Missouri, to Oregon Country.

**province (PRAH-vuhns):** Any one of the large parts some countries, such as Canada, are divided into.

**ratify (RAA-tih-fy):** To formally approve.

**republic (rih-PUHB-lihk):** A country governed by elected representatives and an elected leader.

**reservation (rez-uhr-VAY-shuhn):** Land provided by the U.S. government for a specific Native American group or groups to live on.

# INDEX

**C**

Central Pacific
Railroad, 17
Cherokees, 9
Clark, William, 7
Cleveland, Grover, 21

**G**

Gadsden, James, 17
Gadsden Purchase,
16, 17
Guadalupe Hidalgo,
Treaty of, 15

**J**

Jefferson, Thomas,
6, 7

**L**

Lewis, Meriwether, 7
Liliuokalani, 21
Louisiana Purchase,
6, 7, 8, 11

**M**

McKinley, William, 21

**O**

Oregon Country, 10,
11, 12, 13
Oregon Trail, 10, 11
O'Sullivan, John L.,
5, 22

**P**

Polk, James K., 12,
13, 15

**S**

Santa Anna, Antonio
de, 17
Seward, William,
20, 21
Southern Pacific
Railroad, 17
Spanish-American
War, 18, 19

**T**

Taylor, Zachary, 15
Trail of Tears, 9

**U**

U.S.-Mexican War,
14, 15
Union Pacific
Railroad, 17

# PRIMARY SOURCE LIST

**Cover:** *Westward the Course of Empire Takes Its Way*. Created by Emanuel Gottlieb Leutze. 1861. Oil on canvas. Now kept at the Smithsonian American Art Museum, Washington, D.C.

**Page 4:** *American Progress*. Print, based on original created by John Gast. 1872. Original now kept at the Autry Museum of the American West, Los Angeles, California.

**Page 11:** *Emigrants Crossing the Plains*, or *The Oregon Trail*. Created by Albert Bierstadt. 1869. Oil on canvas. Now kept at the Butler Institute of American Art, Youngstown, Ohio.

**Page 14:** Map of the United States of Mexico. Created by J. Distrunell. 1847. Now kept at the National Archives, Washington, D.C.

# WEBSITES

Due to the changing nature of Internet links, PowerKids Press has developed an online list of websites related to the subject of this book. This site is updated regularly. Please use this link to access the list: www.powerkidslinks.com/soah/mandes